'All nations colors, barbarisms, civilizations, languages . . .'

WALT WHITMAN
Born 1819 West Hills, Long Island
Died 1892 Camden, New Jersey

Leaves of Grass published in many different editions,
with many additional poems, between 1855 and 1892.
This book makes a small selection.

WHITMAN IN PENGUIN CLASSICS
Leaves of Grass
The Complete Poems

WALT WHITMAN

On the Beach at Night Alone

PENGUIN BOOKS

PENGUIN CLASSICS

Published by the Penguin Group
Penguin Books Ltd, 80 Strand, London WC2R ORL, England
Penguin Group (USA) Inc., 375 Hudson Street, New York, New York 10014, USA
Penguin Group (Canada), 90 Eglinton Avenue East, Suite 700, Toronto, Ontario,
Canada M4P 2Y3 (a division of Pearson Penguin Canada Inc.)
Penguin Ireland, 25 St Stephen's Green, Dublin 2, Ireland
(a division of Penguin Books Ltd)
Penguin Group (Australia), 707 Collins Street, Melbourne, Victoria 3008, Australia
(a division of Pearson Australia Group Pty Ltd)
Penguin Books India Pvt Ltd, 11 Community Centre, Panchsheel Park,
New Delhi – 110 017, India
Penguin Group (NZ), 67 Apollo Drive, Rosedale, Auckland 0632, New Zealand
(a division of Pearson New Zealand Ltd)
Penguin Books (South Africa) (Pty) Ltd, Block D, Rosebank Office Park,
181 Jan Smuts Avenue, Parktown North, Gauteng 2193, South Africa

Penguin Books Ltd, Registered Offices: 80 Strand, London WC2R ORL, England

www.penguin.com

This selection published in Penguin Classics 2015
001

Set in 9/12.4 pt Baskerville 10 Pro
Typeset by Jouve (UK), Milton Keynes
Printed in Great Britain by Clays Ltd, St Ives plc

A CIP catalogue record for this book is available from the British Library

ISBN: 978-0-141-39822-8

www.greenpenguin.co.uk

MIX
Paper from
responsible sources
FSC
www.fsc.org   FSC® C018179

Penguin Books is committed to a sustainable
future for our business, our readers and our planet.
This book is made from Forest Stewardship
Council™ certified paper.

Contents

BIRDS OF PASSAGE

Song of the Universal

1

Come said the Muse,
Sing me a song no poet yet has chanted,
Sing me the universal.

In this broad earth of ours,
Amid the measureless grossness and the slag,
Enclosed and safe within its central heart,
Nestles the seed perfection.

By every life a share or more or less,
None born but it is born, conceal'd or unconceal'd the seed
    is waiting.

2

Lo! keen-eyed towering science,
As from tall peaks the modern overlooking,
Successive absolute fiats issuing.

Yet again, lo! the soul, above all science,
For it has history gather'd like husks around the globe,
For it the entire star-myriads roll through the sky.

In spiral routes by long detours,
(As a much-tacking ship upon the sea,)
For it the partial to the permanent flowing;
For it the real to the ideal tends.

For it the mystic evolution,
Not the right only justified, what we call evil also justified.

Forth from their masks, no matter what,
From the huge festering trunk, from craft and guile and
    tears,
Health to emerge and joy, joy universal.
Out of the bulk, the morbid and the shallow,
Out of the bad majority, the varied countless frauds of men
    and states,
Electric, antiseptic yet, cleaving, suffusing all,
Only the good is universal.

3

Over the mountain-growths disease and sorrow,
An uncaught bird is ever hovering, hovering,
High in the purer, happier air.

From imperfection's murkiest cloud,
Darts always forth one ray of perfect light,
One flash of heaven's glory.

To fashion's, custom's discord,
To the mad Babel-din, the deafening orgies,
Soothing each lull a strain is heard, just heard,
From some far shore the final chorus sounding.

O the blest eyes, the happy hearts,
That see, that know the guiding thread so fine,
Along the mighty labyrinth.

4

And thou America,
For the scheme's culmination, its thought and its reality,
For these (not for thyself) thou has arrived.

Thou too surroundest all,
Embracing carrying welcoming all, thou too by pathways
    broad and new,
To the ideal tendest.

The measur'd faiths of other lands, the grandeurs of the
    past,
Are not for thee, but grandeurs of thine own,
Deific faiths and amplitudes, absorbing,
    comprehending all,
All eligible to all.

All, all for immortality,
Love like the light silently wrapping all,
Nature's amelioration blessing all,
The blossoms, fruits of ages, orchards divine and certain,

Walt Whitman

Forms, objects, growths, humanities, to spirtual images
ripening.

Give me O God to sing that thought,
Give me, give him or her I love this quenchless faith,
In Thy ensemble, whatever else withheld withhold not
from us,
Belief in plan of Thee enclosed in Time and Space,
Health, peace, salvation universal.

Is it a dream?
Nay but the lack of it the dream,
And failing it life's lore and wealth a dream,
And all the world a dream.

Pioneers! O Pioneers!

Come my tan-faced children,
Follow well in order, get your weapons ready,
Have you your pistols? have you your sharp-edged axes?
    Pioneers! O pioneers!

For we cannot tarry here,
We must march my darlings, we must bear the brunt of
            danger,
We the youthful sinewy races, all the rest on us depend,
    Pioneers! O pioneers!

O you youths, Western youths,
So impatient, full of action, full of manly pride and
            friendship,
Plain I see you Western youths, see you tramping with the
        foremost,
    Pioneers! O pioneers!

Have the elder races halted?
Do they droop and end their lesson, wearied over there
            beyond the seas?
We take up the task eternal, and the burden and the lesson,
    Pioneers! O pioneers!

All the past we leave behind,
We debouch upon a newer mightier world, varied world,
Fresh and strong the world we seize, world of labor and the
        march,
    Pioneers! O pioneers!

We detachments steady throwing,
Down the edges, through the passes, up the mountains
steep,
Conquering, holding, daring, venturing as we go the
unknown ways,
Pioneers! O pioneers!

We primeval forests felling,
We the rivers stemming, vexing we and piercing deep the
mines within,
We the surface broad surveying, we the virgin soil
upheaving,
Pioneers! O pioneers!

Colorado men are we,
From the peaks gigantic, from the giant sierras and the
high plateaus,
From the mine and from the gully, from the hunting trail
we come,
Pioneers! O pioneers!

From Nebraska, from Arkansas,
Central inland race are we, from Missouri, with the
continental blood intervein'd,
All the hands of comrades clasping, all the Southern, all
the Northern,
Pioneers! O pioneers!

O resistless restless race!
O beloved race in all! O my breast aches with tender love
for all!
O I mourn and yet exult, I am rapt with love for all,
Pioneers! O pioneers!

Raise the mighty mother mistress,
Waving high the delicate mistress, over all the starry
mistress, (bend your heads all,)
Raise the fang'd and warlike mistress, stern, impassive,
weapon'd mistress,
Pioneers! O pioneers!

See my children, resolute children,
By those swarms upon our rear we must never yield or falter,
Ages back in ghostly millions frowning there behind us
urging,
Pioneers! O pioneers!

On and on the compact ranks,
With accessions ever waiting, with the places of the dead
quickly fill'd,
Through the battle, through defeat, moving yet and never
stopping,
Pioneers! O pioneers!

O to die advancing on!
Are there some of us to droop and die? has the hour come?
Then upon the march we fittest die, soon and sure the gap
is fill'd,
Pioneers! O pioneers!

All the pulses of the world,
Falling in they beat for us, with the Western movement
         beat,
Holding single or together, steady moving to the front, all
         for us,
         Pioneers! O pioneers!

Life's involv'd and varied pageants,
All the forms and shows, all the workmen at their work,
All the seamen and the landsmen, all the masters with their
         slaves,
         Pioneers! O pioneers!

All the hapless silent lovers,
All the prisoners in the prisons, all the righteous and the
         wicked,
All the joyous, all the sorrowing, all the living, all the
         dying,
         Pioneers! O pioneers!

I too with my soul and body,
We, a curious trio, picking, wandering on our way,
Through these shores amid the shadows, with the
         apparitions pressing,
         Pioneers! O pioneers!

Lo, the darting bowling orb!
Lo, the brother orbs around, all the clustering suns and
         planets,
All the dazzling days, all the mystic nights with dreams,
         Pioneers! O pioneers!

These are of us, they are with us,
All for primal needed work, while the followers there in
      embryo wait behind,
We to-day's procession heading, we the route for travel
      clearing,
      Pioneers! O pioneers!

O you daughters of the West!
O you young and elder daughters! O you mothers and you
      wives!
Never must you be divided, in our ranks you move united,
      Pioneers! O pioneers!

Minstrels latent on the prairies!
(Shrouded bards of other lands, you may rest, you have
      done your work,)
Soon I hear you coming warbling, soon you rise and tramp
      amid us,
      Pioneers! O pioneers!

Not for delectations sweet,
Not the cushion and the slipper, not the peaceful and the
      studious,
Not the riches safe and palling, not for us the tame enjoyment,
      Pioneers! O pioneers!

Do the feasters gluttonous feast?
Do the corpulent sleepers sleep? have they lock'd and
      bolted doors?
Still be ours the diet hard, and the blanket on the ground,
      Pioneers! O pioneers!

9

Has the night descended?
Was the road of late so toilsome? did we stop discouraged
        nodding on our way?
Yet a passing hour I yield you in your tracks to pause
        oblivious,
    Pioneers! O pioneers!

    Till with sound of trumpet,
Far, far off the daybreak call – hark! how loud and clear I
        hear it wind,
Swift! to the head of the army!–swift! spring to your
        places,
    Pioneers! O pioneers!

To You

Whoever you are, I fear you are walking the walks of
 dreams,
I fear these supposed realities are to melt from under your
 feet and hands,
Even now your features, joys, speech, house, trade,
 manners, troubles, follies, costume, crimes, dissipate
 away from you,
Your true soul and body appear before me,
They stand forth out of affairs, out of commerce, shops,
 work, farms, clothes, the house, buying, selling, eating,
 drinking, suffering, dying.

Whoever you are, now I place my hand upon you, that you
 be my poem,
I whisper with my lips close to your ear,
I have loved many women and men, but I love none better
 than you.

O I have been dilatory and dumb,
I should have made my way straight to you long ago,
I should have blabb'd nothing but you, I should have
 chanted nothing but you.

I will leave all and come and make the hymns of you,
None has understood you, but I understand you,
None has done justice to you, you have not done justice to
 yourself,

Walt Whitman

None but has found you imperfect, I only find no
    imperfection in you,
None but would subordinate you, I only am he who will
    never consent to subordinate you,
I only am he who places over you no master, owner, better,
    God, beyond what waits intrinsically in yourself.

Painters have painted their swarming groups and the
    centre-figure of all,
From the head of the centre-figure spreading a nimbus of
    gold-color'd light,
But I paint myriads of heads, but paint no head without its
    nimbus of gold-color'd light,
From my hand from the brain of every man and woman it
    streams, effulgently flowing forever.
O I could sing such grandeurs and glories about you!
You have not known what you are, you have slumber'd
    upon yourself all your life,
Your eyelids have been the same as closed most of the
    time,
What you have done returns already in mockeries,
(Your thrift, knowledge, prayers, if they do not return in
    mockeries, what is their return?)

The mockeries are not you,
Underneath them and within them I see you lurk,
I pursue you where none else has pursued you,
Silence, the desk, the flippant expression, the night, the
    accustom'd routine, if these conceal you from others or
    from yourself, they do not conceal you from me,

The shaved face, the unsteady eye, the impure complexion,
   if these balk others they do not balk me,
The pert apparel, the deform'd attitude, drunkenness,
   greed, premature death, all these I part aside.

There is no endowment in man or woman that is not tallied
   in you,
There is no virtue, no beauty in man or woman, but as
   good is in you,
No pluck, no endurance in others, but as good is in you,
No pleasure waiting for others, but an equal pleasure waits
   for you.

As for me, I give nothing to any one except I give the like
   carefully to you,
I sing the songs of the glory of none, not God, sooner than
   I sing the songs of the glory of you.

Whoever you are! claim your own at any hazard!
These shows of the East and West are tame compared
   to you,
These immense meadows, these interminable rivers, you are
   immense and interminable as they,
These furies, elements, storms, motions of Nature, throes of
   apparent dissolution, you are he or she who is master or
   mistress over them,
Master or mistress in your own right over Nature, elements,
   pain, passion, dissolution.

The hopples fall from your ankles, you find an unfailing
    sufficiency,
Old or young, male or female, rude, low, rejected by the
    rest, whatever you are promulges itself,
Through birth, life, death, burial, the means are provided,
    nothing is scanted,
Through angers, losses, ambition, ignorance, ennui, what
    you are picks its way.

France, the 18th Year of These States

A great year and place.
A harsh discordant natal scream out-sounding, to touch the
    mother's heart closer than any yet.

I walk'd the shores of my Eastern sea,
Heard over the waves the little voice,
Saw the divine infant where she woke mournfully wailing,
    amid the roar of cannon, curses, shouts, crash of falling
    buildings,
Was not so sick from the blood in the gutters running, nor
    from the single corpses, nor those in heaps, nor those
    borne away in the tumbrils,
Was not so desperate at the battues of death – was not so
    shock'd at the repeated fusillades of the guns.

Pale, silent, stern, what could I say to that long-accrued
    retribution?
Could I wish humanity different?
Could I wish the people made of wood and stone?
Or that there be no justice in destiny or time?

O Liberty! O mate for me!
Here too the blaze, the grape-shot and the axe, in reserve,
    to fetch them out in case of need,
Here too, though long represt, can never be destroy'd,
Here too could rise at last murdering and ecstatic,
Here too demanding full arrears of vengeance.

Hence I sign this salute over the sea,

And I do not deny that terrible red birth and baptism,

But remember the little voice that I heard wailing, and wait
    with perfect trust, no matter how long,

And from to-day sad and cogent I maintain the bequeath'd
    cause, as for all lands,

And I send these words to Paris with my love,

And I guess some chansonniers there will understand them,

For I guess there is latent music yet in France, floods of it,

O I hear already the bustle of instruments, they will soon
    be drowning all that would interrupt them,

O I think the east wind brings a triumphal and free march,

It reaches hither, it swells me to joyful madness,

I will run transpose it in words, to justify it,

I will yet sing a song for you ma femme.

Myself and Mine

Myself and mine gymnastic ever,
To stand the cold or heat, to take good aim with a
    gun, to sail a boat, to manage horses, to beget
    superb children,
To speak readily and clearly, to feel at home among
    common people,
And to hold our own in terrible positions on land and sea.

Not for an embroiderer,
(There will always be plenty of embroiderers, I welcome
    them also,)
But for the fibre of things and for inherent men and
    women.

Not to chisel ornaments,
But to chisel with free stroke the heads and limbs of
    plenteous supreme Gods, that the States may realize
    them walking and talking.
Let me have my own way,
Let others promulge the laws, I will make no account of the
    laws,
Let others praise eminent men and hold up peace, I hold
    up agitation and conflict.
I praise no eminent man, I rebuke to his face the one that
    was thought most worthy.

(Who are you? and what are you secretly guilty of all your
    life?
Will you turn aside all your life? will you grub and chatter
    all your life?
And who are you, blabbing by rote, years, pages,
    languages, reminiscences,
Unwitting to-day that you do not know how to speak
    properly a single word?)

Let others finish specimens, I never finish specimens,
I start them by exhaustless laws as Nature does, fresh and
    modern continually.

I give nothing as duties,
What others give as duties I give as living impulses,
(Shall I give the heart's action as a duty?)

Let others dispose of questions, I dispose of nothing, I
    arouse unanswerable questions,
Who are they I see and touch, and what about them?
What about these likes of myself that draw me so close by
    tender directions and indirections?

I call to the world to distrust the accounts of my friends,
    but listen to my enemies, as I myself do,
I charge you forever reject those who would expound me,
    for I cannot expound myself,
I charge that there be no theory or school founded out
    of me,
I charge you to leave all free, as I have left all free.
After me, vista!
O I see life is not short, but immeasurably long,

I henceforth tread the world chaste, temperate, an early
    riser, a steady grower,
Every hour the semen of centuries, and still of centuries.

I must follow up these continual lessons of the air, water,
    earth,
I perceive I have no time to lose.

Year of Meteors (1859–60)

Year of meteors! brooding year!
I would bind in words retrospective some of your deeds
    and signs,
I would sing your contest for the 19th Presidentiad,
I would sing how an old man, tall, with white hair,
    mounted the scaffold in Virginia,
(I was at hand, silent I stood with teeth shut close, I
    watch'd,
I stood very near you old man when cool and indifferent,
    but trembling with age and your unheal'd wounds you
    mounted the scaffold;)
I would sing in my copious song your census returns of the
    States,
The tables of population and products, I would sing of
    your ships and their cargoes,
The proud black ships of Manhattan arriving, some fill'd
    with immigrants, some from the isthmus with cargoes
    of gold,
Songs thereof would I sing, to all that hitherward comes
    would I welcome give,
And you would I sing, fair stripling! welcome to you from
    me, young prince of England!
(Remember you surging Manhattan's crowds as you pass'd
    with your cortege of nobles?
There in the crowds stood I, and singled you out with
    attachment;)

Nor forget I to sing of the wonder, the ship as she swam up
    my bay,

Well-shaped and stately the Great Eastern swam up my
    bay, she was 600 feet long,

Her moving swiftly surrounded by myriads of small craft I
    forget not to sing;

Nor the comet that came unannounced out of the north
    flaring in heaven,

Nor the strange huge meteor-procession dazzling and clear
    shooting over our heads,

(A moment, a moment long it sail'd its balls of unearthly
    light over our heads,

Then departed, dropt in the night, and was gone;)

Of such, and fitful as they, I sing – with gleams from them
    would I gleam and patch these chants,

Your chants, O year all mottled with evil and good – year
    of forebodings!

Year of comets and meteors transient and strange – lo! even
    here one equally transient and strange!

As I flit through you hastily, soon to fall and be gone, what
    is this chant,

What am I myself but one of your meteors?

With Antecedents

1

With antecedents,

With my fathers and mothers and the accumulations of past
ages,

With all which, had it not been, I would not now be here,
as I am,

With Egypt, India, Phenicia, Greece and Rome,

With the Kelt, the Scandinavian, the Alb and the Saxon,

With antique maritime ventures, laws, artisanship, wars
and journeys,

With the poet, the skald, the saga, the myth, and the
oracle,

With the sale of slaves, with enthusiasts, with the
troubadour, the crusader, and the monk,

With those old continents whence we have come to this
new continent,

With the fading kingdoms and kings over there,

With the fading religions and priests,

With the small shores we look back to from our own large
and present shores,

With countless years drawing themselves onward and
arrived at these years,

You and me arrived – America arrived and making this
year,

This year! sending itself ahead countless years to come.

2

O but it is not the years – it is I, it is You,
We touch all laws and tally all antecedents,
We are the skald, the oracle, the monk and the knight, we
easily include them and more,
We stand amid time beginningless and endless, we stand
amid evil and good,
All swings around us, there is as much darkness as light,
The very sun swings itself and its system of planets
around us,
Its sun, and its again, all swing around us.

As for me, (torn, stormy, amid these vehement days,)
I have the idea of all, and am all and believe in all,
I believe materialism is true and spiritualism is true, I reject
no part.

(Have I forgotten any part? any thing in the past?
Come to me whoever and whatever, till I give you
recognition.)

I respect Assyria, China, Teutonia, and the Hebrews,
I adopt each theory, myth, god, and demi-god,
I see that the old accounts, bibles, genealogies, are true,
without exception,
I assert that all past days were what they must have been,
And that they could no-how have been better than they
were,

And that to-day is what it must be, and that America is,
And that to-day and America could no-how be better than
    they are.

3

In the name of these States and in your and my name, the
    Past,
And in the name of these States and in your and my name,
    the Present time.

I know that the past was great and the future will be great,
And I know that both curiously conjoint in the present
    time,
(For the sake of him I typify, for the common average man's
    sake, your sake if you are he,)
And that where I am or you are this present day, there is the
    centre of all days, all races,
And there is the meaning to us of all that has ever come of
    races and days, or ever will come.

A Broadway Pageant

1

Over the Western sea hither from Niphon come,
Courteous, the swart-cheek'd two-sworded envoys,
Leaning back in their open barouches, bare-headed,
    impassive,
Ride to-day through Manhattan.

Libertad! I do not know whether others behold what I
    behold,
In the procession along with the nobles of Niphon, the
    errand-bearers,
Bringing up the rear, hovering above, around, or in the
    ranks marching,
But I will sing you a song of what I behold Libertad.
When million-footed Manhattan unpent descends to her
    pavements,
When the thunder-cracking guns arouse me with the proud
    roar I love,
When the round-mouth'd guns out of the smoke and smell
    I love spit their salutes,
When the fire-flashing guns have fully alerted me,
    and heaven-clouds canopy my city with a delicate
    thin haze,
When gorgeous the countless straight stems, the forests at
    the wharves, thicken with colors,
When every ship richly drest carries her flag at the peak,

When pennants trail and street-festoons hang from the
   windows,
When Broadway is entirely given up to foot-passengers and
   foot-standers, when the mass is densest,
When the façades of the houses are alive with people, when
   eyes gaze riveted tens of thousands at a time,
When the guests from the islands advance, when the
   pageant moves forward visible,
When the summons is made, when the answer that waited
   thousands of years answers,
I too arising, answering, descend to the pavements, merge
   with the crowd, and gaze with them.

2

Superb-faced Manhattan!
Comrade Americanos! to us, then at last the Orient comes.

To us, my city,
Where our tall-topt marble and iron beauties range on
   opposite sides, to walk in the space between,
To-day our Antipodes comes.

The Originatress comes,
The nest of languages, the bequeather of poems, the race
   of eld,
Florid with blood, pensive, rapt with musings, hot with
   passion,
Sultry with perfume, with ample and flowing garments,

With sunburnt visage, with intense soul and glittering
    eyes,
The race of Brahma comes.

See my cantabile! these and more are flashing to us from
    the procession,
As it moves changing, a kaleidoscope divine it moves
    changing before us.

For not the envoys nor the tann'd Japanee from his island
    only,
Lithe and silent the Hindoo appears, the Asiatic continent
    itself appears, the past, the dead,
The murky night-morning of wonder and fable inscrutable,
The envelop'd mysteries, the old and unknown hive-bees,
The north, the sweltering south, eastern Assyria, the
    Hebrews, the ancient of ancients,
Vast desolated cities, the gliding present, all of these and
    more are in the pageant-procession.

Geography, the world, is in it,
The Great Sea, the brood of islands, Polynesia, the coast
    beyond,
The coast you henceforth are facing – you Libertad! from
    your Western golden shores,
The countries there with their populations, the millions
    en-masse are curiously here,
The swarming market-places, the temples with idols ranged
    along the sides or at the end, bonze, brahmin, and
    llama,
Mandarin, farmer, merchant, mechanic, and fisherman,

The singing-girl and the dancing-girl, the ecstatic persons,
    the secluded emperors,
Confucious himself, the great poets and heroes, the
    warriors, the castes, all,
Trooping up, crowding from all directions, from the Altay
    mountains,
From Thibet, from the four winding and far-flowing rivers
    of China,
From the southern peninsulas and the demi-continental
    islands, from Malaysia,
These and whatever belongs to them palpable show forth
    to me, and are seiz'd by me,
And I am seiz'd by them, and friendlily held by them,
Till as here them all I chant, Libertad! for themselves and
    for you.

For I too raising my voice join the ranks of this pageant,
I am the chanter, I chant aloud over the pageant,
I chant the world on my Western sea,
I chant copious the islands beyond, thick as stars in
    the sky,
I chant the new empire grander than any before, as in a
    vision it comes to me,
I chant America the mistress, I chant a greater supremacy,
I chant projected a thousand blooming cities yet in time on
    those groups of sea-islands,
My sail-ships and steam-ships threading the archipelagoes,
My stars and stripes fluttering in the wind,
Commerce opening, the sleep of ages having done its work,
    races reborn, refresh'd,

Lives, works resumed – the object I know not – but the
    old, the Asiatic renew'd as it must be,
Commencing from this day surrounded by the world.

3

And you Libertad of the world!
You shall sit in the middle well-pois'd thousands and
    thousands of years,
As to-day from one side the nobles of Asia come to you,
As to-morrow from the other side the queen of England
    sends her eldest son to you.

The sign is reversing, the orb is enclosed,
The ring is circled, the journey is done,
The box-lid is but perceptibly open'd, nevertheless the
    perfume pours copiously out of the whole box.
Young Libertad! with the venerable Asia, the all-mother,
Be considerate with her now and ever hot Libertad, for you
    are all,
Bend your proud neck to the long-off mother now sending
    messages over the archipelagoes to you,
Bend your proud neck low for once, young Libertad.

Were the children straying westward so long? so wide the
    tramping?
Were the precedent dim ages debouching westward from
    Paradise so long?
Were the centuries steadily footing it that way, all the while
    unknown, for you, for reasons?

Walt Whitman

They are justified, they are accomplish'd, they shall now
be turn'd the other way also, to travel toward you
thence,
They shall now also march obediently eastward for your
sake Libertad.

SEA-DRIFT

Out of the Cradle Endlessly Rocking

Out of the cradle endlessly rocking,
Out of the mocking-bird's throat, the musical shuttle,
Out of the Ninth-month midnight,
Over the sterile sands and the fields beyond, where the
    child leaving his bed wander'd alone, bareheaded,
    barefoot,
Down from the shower'd halo,
Up from the mystic play of shadows twining and twisting
    as if they were alive,
Out from the patches of briers and blackberries,
From the memories of the bird that chanted to me,
From your memories sad brother, from the fitful risings and
    fallings I heard,
From under that yellow half-moon late-risen and swollen as
    if with tears,
From those beginning notes of yearning and love there in
    the mist,
From the thousand responses of my heart never to cease,
From the myriad thence-arous'd words,
From the word stronger and more delicious than any,
From such as now they start the scene revisiting,
As a flock, twittering, rising, or overhead passing,

Borne hither, ere all eludes me, hurriedly,
A man, yet by these tears a little boy again,
Throwing myself on the sand, confronting the waves,
I, chanter of pains and joys, uniter of here and hereafter,
Taking all hints to use them, but swiftly leaping beyond them,
A reminiscence sing.

Once Paumanok,
When the lilac-scent was in the air and Fifth-month grass
    was growing,
Up this seashore in some briers,
Two feather'd guests from Alabama, two together,
And their nest, and four light-green eggs spotted with
    brown,
And every day the he-bird to and fro near at hand,
And every day the she-bird crouch'd on her nest, silent,
    with bright eyes,
And every day I, a curious boy, never too close, never
    disturbing them,
Cautiously peering, absorbing, translating.

Shine! shine! shine!
Pour down your warmth, great sun!
While we bask, we two together.

Two together!
Winds blow south, or winds blow north,
Day come white, or night come black,
Home, or rivers and mountains from home,
Singing all time, minding no time,
While we two keep together.

Till of a sudden,
May-be kill'd, unknown to her mate,
One forenoon the she-bird crouch'd not on the nest,
Nor return'd that afternoon, nor the next,
Nor ever appear'd again.

And thenceforward all summer in the sound of the sea,
And at night under the full of the moon in calmer
    weather,
Over the hoarse surging of the sea,
Or flitting from brier to brier by day,
I saw, I heard at intervals the remaining one, the he-bird,
The solitary guest from Alabama.

Blow! blow! blow!
Blow up sea-winds along Paumanok's shore;
I wait and I wait till you blow my mate to me.

Yes, when the stars glisten'd,
All night long on the prong of a moss-scallop'd stake,
Down almost amid the slapping waves,
Sat the lone singer wonderful causing tears.
He call'd on his mate,
He pour'd forth the meanings which I of all men know.

Yes my brother I know,
The rest might not, but I have treasur'd every note,
For more than once dimly down to the beach gliding,
Silent, avoiding the moonbeams, blending myself with the
    shadows,
Recalling now the obscure shapes, the echoes, the sounds
    and sights after their sorts,

33

The white arms out in the breakers tirelessly tossing,
I, with bare feet, a child, the wind wafting my hair,
Listen'd long and long.

Listen'd to keep, to sing, now translating the notes,
Following you my brother.

Soothe! soothe! soothe!
Close on its wave soothes the wave behind,
And again another behind embracing and lapping, every one
    close,
But my love soothes not me, not me.

Low hangs the moon, it rose late,
It is lagging – O I think it is heavy with love, with love.

O madly the sea pushes upon the land,
With love, with love.

O night! do I not see my love fluttering out among the
    breakers?
What is that little black thing I see there in the white?

Loud! loud! loud!
Loud I call to you, my love!
High and clear I shoot my voice over the waves,
Surely you must know who is here, is here,
You must know who I am, my love.
Low-hanging moon!
What is that dusky spot in your brown yellow?
O it is the shape, the shape of my mate!
O moon do not keep her from me any longer.

Land! land! O land!
Whichever way I turn, O I think you could give me my mate back
*   again if you only would,*
For I am almost sure I see her dimly whichever way I look.

O rising stars!
Perhaps the one I want so much will rise, will rise with some
*   of you.*

O throat! O trembling throat!
Sound clearer through the atmosphere!
Pierce the woods, the earth,
Somewhere listening to catch you must be the one I want.

Shake out carols!
Solitary here, the night's carols!
Carols of lonesome love! death's carols!
Carols under that lagging, yellow, waning moon!
O under that moon where she droops almost down into the sea!
O reckless despairing carols.

But soft! sink low!
Soft! let me just murmur,
And do you wait a moment you husky-nois'd sea,
For somewhere I believe I heard my mate responding to me,
So faint, I must be still, be still to listen,
But not altogether still, for then she might not come immediately
*   to me.*

Walt Whitman

Hither my love!
Here I am! here!
With this just-sustain'd note I announce myself to you,
This gentle call is for you my love, for you.
Do not be decoy'd elsewhere,
That is the whistle of the wind, it is not my voice,
That is the fluttering, the fluttering of the spray,
Those are the shadows of leaves.

O darkness! O in vain!
O I am very sick and sorrowful.

O brown halo in the sky near the moon, drooping upon the sea!
O troubled reflection in the sea!
O throat! O throbbing heart!
And I singing uselessly, uselessly all the night.

O past! O happy life! O songs of joy!
In the air, in the woods, over fields,
Loved! loved! loved! loved! loved!
But my mate no more, no more with me!
We two together no more.

The aria sinking,
All else continuing, the stars shining,
The winds blowing, the notes of the bird continuous
     echoing,
With angry moans the fierce old mother incessantly
     moaning,
On the sands of Paumanok's shore gray and rustling,
The yellow half-moon enlarged, sagging down, drooping,
     the face of the sea almost touching,

The boy ecstatic, with his bare feet the waves, with his hair
    the atmosphere dallying,
The love in the heart long pent, now loose, now at last
    tumultuously bursting,
The aria's meaning, the ears, the soul, swiftly depositing,
The strange tears down the cheeks coursing,
The colloquy there, the trio, each uttering,
The undertone, the savage old mother incessantly crying,
To the boy's soul's questions sullenly timing, some drown'd
    secret hissing,
To the outsetting bard.
Demon or bird! (said the boy's soul,)
Is it indeed toward your mate you sing? or is it really
    to me?
For I, that was a child, my tongue's use sleeping, now I
    have heard you,
Now in a moment I know what I am for, I awake,
And already a thousand singers, a thousand songs, clearer,
    louder and more sorrowful than yours,
A thousand warbling echoes have started to life within me,
    never to die.

O you singer solitary, singing by yourself, projecting me,
O solitary me listening, never more shall I cease
    perpetuating you,
Never more shall I escape, never more the reverberations,
Never more the cries of unsatisfied love be absent from me,
Never again leave me to be the peaceful child I was before
    what there in the night,
By the sea under the yellow and sagging moon,

The messenger there arous'd, the fire, the sweet hell within,
The unknown want, the destiny of me.

O give me the clew! (it lurks in the night here
    somewhere,)
O if I am to have so much, let me have more!

A word then, (for I will conquer it,)
The word final, superior to all,
Subtle, sent up – what is it? – I listen;
Are you whispering it, and have been all the time, you
    sea-waves?
Is that it from your liquid rims and wet sands?

Whereto answering, the sea,
Delaying not, hurrying not,
Whisper'd me through the night, and very plainly before
    daybreak,
Lisp'd to me the low and delicious word death,
And again death, death, death, death,
Hissing melodious, neither like the bird nor like my arous'd
    child's heart,
But edging near as privately for me rustling at my feet,
Creeping thence steadily up to my ears and laving me softly
    all over,
Death, death, death, death, death.

Which I do not forget,
But fuse the song of my dusky demon and brother,
That he sang to me in the moonlight on Paumanok's gray
    beach,
With the thousand responsive songs at random,

My own songs awaked from that hour,
And with them the key, the word up from the waves,
The word of the sweetest song and all songs,
That strong and delicious word which, creeping to my feet,
(Or like some old crone rocking the cradle, swathed in
    sweet garments, bending aside,)
The sea whisper'd me.

As I Ebb'd with the Ocean of Life

1

As I ebb'd with the ocean of life,
As I wended the shores I know,
As I walk'd where the ripples continually wash you
    Paumanok,
Where they rustle up hoarse and sibilant,
Where the fierce old mother endlessly cries for her
    castaways,
I musing late in the autumn day, gazing off southward,
Held by this electric self out of the pride of which I utter
    poems,
Was seiz'd by the spirit that trails in the lines underfoot,
The rim, the sediment that stands for all the water and all
    the land of the globe.

Fascinated, my eyes reverting from the south, dropt, to
    follow those slender windrows,
Chaff, straw, splinters of wood, weeds, and the sea-gluten,
Scum, scales from shining rocks, leaves of salt-lettuce, left
    by the tide,
Miles walking, the sound of breaking waves the other side
    of me,
Paumanok there and then as I thought the old thought of
    likenesses,
These you presented to me you fish-shaped island,

As I wended the shores I know,
As I walk'd with that electric self seeking types.

2

As I wend to the shores I know not,
As I list to the dirge, the voices of men and women wreck'd,
As I inhale the impalpable breezes that set in upon me,
As the ocean so mysterious rolls toward me closer and
    closer,
I too but signify at the utmost a little wash'd-up drift,
A few sands and dead leaves to gather,
Gather, and merge myself as part of the sands and drift.

O baffled, balk'd, bent to the very earth,
Oppress'd with myself that I have dared to open my
    mouth,
Aware now that amid all that blab whose echoes recoil
    upon me I have not once had the least idea who or
    what I am,
But that before all my arrogant poems the real Me stands
    yet untouch'd, untold, altogether unreach'd,
Withdrawn far, mocking me with mock-congratulatory
    signs and bows,
With peals of distant ironical laughter at every word I have
    written,
Pointing in silence to these songs, and then to the sand
    beneath.

I perceive I have not really understood any thing, not a
    single object, and that no man ever can,
Nature here in sight of the sea taking advantage of me to
    dart upon me and sting me,
Because I have dared to open my mouth to sing at all.

3

You oceans both, I close with you,
We murmur alike reproachfully rolling sands and drift,
    knowing not why,
These little shreds indeed standing for you and me and all.

You friable shore with trails of debris,
You fish-shaped island, I take what is underfoot,
What is yours is mine my father.

I too Paumanok,
I too have bubbled up, floated the measureless float, and
    been wash'd on your shores,
I too am but a trail of drift and debris,
I too leave little wrecks upon you, you fish-shaped island.

I throw myself upon your breast my father,
I cling to you so that you cannot unloose me,
I hold you so firm till you answer me something.

Kiss me my father,
Touch me with your lips as I touch those I love,
Breathe to me while I hold you close the secret of the
    murmuring I envy.

4

Ebb, ocean of life, (the flow will return,)
Cease not your moaning you fierce old mother,
Endlessly cry for your castaways, but fear not, deny
    not me,
Rustle not up so hoarse and angry against my feet as I
    touch you or gather from you.

I mean tenderly by you and all,
I gather for myself and for this phantom looking down
    where we lead, and following me and mine.

Me and mine, loose windrows, little corpses,
Froth, snowy white, and bubbles,
(See, from my dead lips the ooze exuding at last,
See, the prismatic colors glistening and rolling,)
Tufts of straw, sands, fragments,
Buoy'd hither from many moods, one contradicting
    another,
From the storm, the long calm, the darkness, the swell,
Musing, pondering, a breath, a briny tear, a dab of liquid
    or soil,
Up just as much out of fathomless workings fermented and
    thrown,
A limp blossom or two, torn, just as much over waves
    floating, drifted at random,
Just as much for us that sobbing dirge of Nature,
Just as much whence we come that blare of the
    cloud-trumpets,

Walt Whitman

We, capricious, brought hither we know not whence,
　　spread out before you,
You up there walking or sitting,
Whoever you are, we too lie in drifts at your feet.

Tears

Tears! tears! tears!
In the night, in solitude, tears,
On the white shore dripping, dripping, suck'd in by the
sand,
Tears, not a star shining, all dark and desolate,
Moist tears from the eyes of a muffled head;
O who is that ghost? that form in the dark, with tears?
What shapeless lump is that, bent, crouch'd there on the
sand?
Streaming tears, sobbing tears, throes, choked with wild
cries;
O storm, embodied, rising, careering with swift steps along
the beach!
O wild and dismal night storm, with wind – O belching
and desperate!
O shade so sedate and decorous by day, with calm
countenance and regulated pace,
But away at night as you fly, none looking – O then the
unloosen'd ocean,
Of tears! tears! tears!

To the Man-of-War Bird

Thou who hast slept all night upon the storm,
Waking renew'd on thy prodigious pinions,
(Burst the wild storm? above it thou ascended'st,
And rested on the sky, thy slave that cradled thee,)
Now a blue point, far, far, in heaven floating,
As to the light emerging here on deck I watch thee,
(Myself a speck, a point on the world's floating vast.)

Far, far at sea,
After the night's fierce drifts have strewn the shore with
     wrecks,
With re-appearing day as now so happy and serene,
The rosy and elastic dawn, the flashing sun,
The limpid spread of air cerulean,
Thou also re-appearest.
Thou born to match the gale, (thou art all wings,)
To cope with heaven and earth and sea and hurricane,
Thou ship of air that never furl'st thy sails,
Days, even weeks untired and onward, through spaces,
     realms gyrating,
At dusk that look'st on Senegal, at morn America,
That sport'st amid the lightning-flash and thunder-cloud,
In them, in thy experiences, had'st thou my soul,
What joys! what joys were thine!

Aboard at a Ship's Helm

Aboard at a ship's helm,
A young steersman steering with care.

Through fog on a sea-coast dolefully ringing,
An ocean-bell – O a warning bell, rock'd by the waves.

O you give good notice indeed, you bell by the sea-reefs
   ringing,
Ringing, ringing, to warn the ship from its wreck-place.

For as on the alert O steersman, you mind the loud
   admonition,
The bows turn, the freighted ship tacking speeds away
   under her gray sails,
The beautiful and noble ship with all her precious wealth
   speeds away gayly and safe.

But O the ship, the immortal ship! O ship aboard the ship!
Ship of the body, ship of the soul, voyaging, voyaging,
   voyaging.

On the Beach at Night

On the beach at night,
Stands a child with her father,
Watching the east, the autumn sky.

Up through the darkness,
While ravening clouds, the burial clouds, in black masses
    spreading,
Lower sullen and fast athwart and down the sky,
Amid a transparent clear belt of ether yet left in the east,
Ascends large and calm the lord-star Jupiter,
And nigh at hand, only a very little above,
Swim the delicate sisters the Pleiades.
From the beach the child holding the hand of her father,
Those burial-clouds that lower victorious soon to
    devour all,
Watching, silently weeps.

Weep not, child,
Weep not, my darling,
With these kisses let me remove your tears,
The ravening clouds shall not long be victorious,
They shall not long possess the sky, they devour the stars
    only in apparition,
Jupiter shall emerge, be patient, watch again another night,
    the Pleiades shall emerge,
They are immortal, all those stars both silvery and golden
    shall shine out again,

The great stars and the little ones shall shine out again, they
    endure,
The vast immortal suns and the long-enduring pensive
    moons shall again shine.

Then dearest child mournest thou only for Jupiter?
Considerest thou alone the burial of the stars?

Something there is,
(With my lips soothing thee, adding I whisper,
I give thee the first suggestion, the problem and
    indirection,)
Something there is more immortal even than the stars,
(Many the burials, many the days and nights, passing
    away,)
Something that shall endure longer even than lustrous
    Jupiter,
Longer than sun or any revolving satellite,
Or the radiant sisters the Pleiades.

The World Below the Brine

The world below the brine,
Forests at the bottom of the sea, the branches and leaves,
Sea-lettuce, vast lichens, strange flowers and seeds, the
    thick tangle, openings, and pink turf,
Different colors, pale gray and green, purple, white, and
    gold, the play of light through the water,
Dumb swimmers there among the rocks, coral, gluten,
    grass, rushes, and the aliment of the swimmers,
Sluggish existences grazing there suspended, or slowly
    crawling close to the bottom,
The sperm-whale at the surface blowing air and spray, or
    disporting with his flukes,
The leaden-eyed shark, the walrus, the turtle, the hairy
    sea-leopard, and the sting-ray,
Passions there, wars, pursuits, tribes, sight in those
    ocean-depths, breathing that thick-breathing air, as so
    many do,
The change thence to the sight here, and to the subtle air
    breathed by beings like us who walk this sphere,
The change onward from ours to that of beings who walk
    other spheres.

On the Beach at Night Alone

On the beach at night alone,
As the old mother sways her to and fro singing her husky
    song,
As I watch the bright stars shining, I think a thought of the
    clef of the universes and of the future.

A vast similitude interlocks all,
All spheres, grown, ungrown, small, large, suns, moons,
    planets,
All distances of place however wide,
All distances of time, all inanimate forms,
All souls, all living bodies though they be ever so different,
    or in different worlds,
All gaseous, watery, vegetable, mineral processes, the
    fishes, the brutes,
All nations, colors, barbarisms, civilizations, languages,
All identities that have existed or may exist on this globe,
    or any globe,
All lives and deaths, all of the past, present, future,
This vast similitude spans them, and always has spann'd,
And shall forever span them and compactly hold and
    enclose them.

Song for All Seas, All Ships

1

To-day a rude brief recitative,
Of ships sailing the seas, each with its special flag or
    ship-signal,
Of unnamed heroes in the ships – of waves spreading and
    spreading far as the eye can reach,
Of dashing spray, and the winds piping and blowing,
And out of these a chant for the sailors of all nations,
Fitful, like a surge.

Of sea-captains young or old, and the mates, and of all
    intrepid sailors,
Of the few, very choice, taciturn, whom fate can never
    surprise nor death dismay,
Pick'd sparingly without noise by thee old ocean, chosen by
    thee,
Thou sea that pickest and cullest the race in time, and
    unitest nations,
Suckled by thee, old husky nurse, embodying thee,
Indomitable, untamed as thee.

(Ever the heroes on water or on land, by ones or twos
    appearing,
Ever the stock preserv'd and never lost, though rare,
    enough for seed preserv'd.)

2

Flaunt out O sea your separate flags of nations!
Flaunt out visible as ever the various ship-signals!
But do you reserve especially for yourself and for the soul
    of man one flag above all the rest,
A spiritual woven signal for all nations, emblem of man
    elate above death,
Token of all brave captains and all intrepid sailors and
    mates,
And all that went down doing their duty,
Reminiscent of them, twined from all intrepid captains
    young or old,
A pennant universal, subtly waving all time, o'er all brave
    sailors,
All seas, all ships.

Patroling Barnegat

Wild, wild the storm, and the sea high running,
Steady the roar of the gale, with incessant undertone
    muttering,
Shouts of demoniac laughter fitfully piercing and pealing,
Waves, air, midnight, their savagest trinity lashing,
Out in the shadows there milk-white combs careering,
On beachy slush and sand spirts of snow fierce slanting,
Where through the murk the easterly death-wind breasting,
Through cutting swirl and spray watchful and firm
    advancing,
(That in the distance! is that a wreck? is the red signal
    flaring?)
Slush and sand of the beach tireless till daylight wending,
Steadily, slowly, through hoarse roar never remitting,
Along the midnight edge by those milk-white combs
    careering,
A group of dim, weird forms, struggling, the night
    confronting,
That savage trinity warily watching.

After the Sea-Ship

After the sea-ship, after the whistling winds,
After the white-gray sails taut to their spars and ropes,
Below, a myriad myriad waves hastening, lifting up their
    necks,
Tending in ceaseless flow toward the track of the ship,
Waves of the ocean bubbling and gurgling, blithely prying,
Waves, undulating waves, liquid, uneven, emulous waves,
Toward that whirling current, laughing and buoyant, with
    curves,
Where the great vessel sailing and tacking displaces the
    surface,
Larger and smaller waves in the spread of the ocean
    yearnfully flowing,
The wake of the sea-ship after she passes, flashing and
    frolicsome under the sun,
A motley procession with many a fleck of foam and many
    fragments,
Following the stately and rapid ship, in the wake following.